THE BROOK DRIED UP

WHY DO CHRISTIANS SUFFER?

Some of the most dramatic and adventurous stories in the Bible revolve around the meteoric rise of Elijah the prophet. Like a shooting star he flashed out of obscurity and changed the character of a whole nation in a very short time.

Little is known about the background of this colorful reformer of Israel. Called of God from the rugged mountains of Gilead, he walked into the palace of King Ahab while apostasy was at its darkest point. Fired by a holy indignation, he confronted the wicked ruler of Israel with words of judgment, "There shall not be dew nor rain these years, but according to my word." 1 Kings 17:1.

After delivering his inspired message, the courageous prophet was commanded by God to hide himself in the eastern wilderness by the brook Cherith. There God arranged providentially for ravens to deliver food to the isolated fugitive during the predicted years of famine.

As the land baked and cracked under the withering heat of the sun, every green plant died for lack of water. But Elijah was well supplied, morning and evening, by the miraculous ministry of the ravens. In addition to the bread and flesh brought by the birds, God provided plenty of refreshing water from the splashing brook which flowed nearby.

What a perfect picture of God's power and willingness to care for the physical needs of His faithful servant! With pleasure we contemplate that scene of restful abundance. The prophet had no problems. Everywhere else the people were suffering from the terror of the

draught, but God would not let His obe-
dient child lack for anything. Without
fail, the ravens flew in twice a day with
their fare of food and the brook was
always yielding its life-giving supply of
water.

Haven't we seen the same kind of
providence in our own day? The God of
Elijah still takes care of the needs of His
children. The prophet was walking in the
center of God's will, and the promised
blessings never failed. Or did they?

Let's read on in the biblical account:
"And the ravens brought him bread and
flesh in the morning, and bread and flesh
in the evening; and he drank of the brook.
And it came to pass after a while, that the
brook dried up." 1 Kings 17:6, 7.

Can't you picture the shock and disappointment as Elijah walked out to the
brook to get his daily water supply? He
looked down upon the dry, brown stones
of the brook-bed and could scarcely believe what he saw. Not a drop of water
remained. A terrible tragedy had over-

taken him—THE BROOK HAD DRIED UP!

We have no way of knowing how long God tested His prophet by the barren brook. For a time, at least, Elijah had to wait in faith. It probably seemed that all the promises were failing. God had abandoned him to an agonizing death in the parched wilderness. But as he lingered and listened, God spoke these words, "Arise, get thee to Zarephath, which belongeth to Zidon, and dwell there: behold, I have commanded a widow woman there to sustain thee." 1 Kings 17:9.

Don't you see how God closed one door so that He could open another one? Elijah had been there long enough. God had another experience waiting for him in Zarephath. God provided the brook, and God dried it up. It would have been a tragedy for the prophet to remain longer in the wilderness. Life was moving on. In the dynamics of divine Providence, Elijah was scheduled to experience another miracle in another place. Had the brook not dried up, he would have stayed there. He would have relaxed in the satisfying fullness of material blessing. But he would have missed the widow's cruse, the Carmel experience, and Elisha plowing in the field.

Listen, God's brooks always dry up. He doesn't want us to stay in the same place all the time. That is our great problem. We get by our comfortable brook, surrounded by peaceful plenty, and want to rest there the remainder of our days. Then when God allows the brook to dry up, we often weep and blame God for afflicting us.

Let me ask you, was Elijah backsliding when the brook dried up on him? No, he was growing spiritually. Zarephath was many times more wonderful than Cherith. But please take note that God closed up Cherith before He revealed Zarephath. Faith had to be tested. There is always the time when everything looks absolutely hopeless. It happened with Elijah and it will happen to us.

The Eternal "Why?"

Almost daily I stand with people beside their dried-up brooks trying to help them see that the world has not come to an end. One of the hardest questions for a minister to answer is "Why?" Why did my baby die? Why did I lose my job? Why are my children so unconcerned about spiritual things? Why did my companion abandon me for another?

Under the emotional stress of our loss we tend to blame God for making some terrible mistakes in dealing with our lives. It is so human to do this because we have no way of seeing the future.

I can still remember weeping, as a child, when I read the story of Joseph for the first time. He had been so happy and carefree. Then, suddenly, his brook dried up. He was on the way to Egypt as a slave. How Jacob grieved for that lost boy! We can hear him moaning, "Simeon is not and Joseph is gone. Now you want to take Benjamin from me. Everything is against me." Genesis 42:36.

How familiar it sounds. Poor Jacob couldn't see through the "whys" any more than we can. But a little while later we see him on his camel, hurrying toward Egypt. His heart was overflowing with joy. Another brook had broken forth in his life. And then we hear Joseph saying to his brothers, "Ye thought evil against me: but God meant it unto good." Genesis 50:20.

It is so easy to look back as Joseph did that day and confess that the disappointments have really been His appointments. Why can't we have the faith to stand by our dried-up brooks and make that confession? Someday in the future every redeemed soul will do it in retrospect. God delights in those who will take Him at His word and claim the promise of Romans 8:28 even while the heart is breaking with sorrow. "All things work together for good to them that love God, to them who are the called according to his purpose."

The Fires of Affliction

The Bible is laced with texts about the spiritual benefits of suffering. Peter said to "think it not strange concerning the fiery trial which is to try you, as though some strange thing happened unto you." 1 Peter 4:12. Paul assures us that "all that will live godly in Christ Jesus shall suffer persecution." 2 Timothy 3:12. And James makes the incredible statement, "Count it all joy when ye fall into divers temptations; Knowing this, that the trying of your faith worketh patience." James 1:2, 3.

In the light of these and many more similar statements, we must confess that there are mysterious blessings associated with trials and suffering. James indicates that they develop the very character traits which mark those who will be candidates for the Kingdom. In Revelation the saints are described in these words: "Here is the patience of the saints: here are they that keep the commandments of God, and the faith of Jesus." Revelation 14:12.

Obviously, patience is a requirement for those who are redeemed out of this world. James says that patience is developed by tests and trials. This clearly teaches us that suffering may indeed be a necessary molding process in our preparation for heaven.

David, who also suffered much, came to this amazing conclusion: "It is good for me that I have been afflicted; that I might learn thy statutes." Psalms 119:71. Again, he wrote, "Before I was afflicted I went astray." Psalm 119:67.

Until a Christian learns this simple Bible principle, he will live in a ferment of doubt and uncertainty. Every experience of disappointment will raise fresh questions concerning God's justice and love. Many Christians hold the childish view that because we have accepted Jesus and because He loves us, therefore, He will use His mighty power to preserve us from every pain and trial.

The inspired record reveals that because He loves us, He will often permit us to pass through the fires of affliction. Why does He do it? Because He sees that this is the only way to prepare us to be with Him for eternity. God is actually answering the prayers of those who have asked for purification of life. When we pray for God to eradicate sin from our life, we must be ready to accept His ordained method of accomplishing that work. Grinding trials appear to be part of the machinery by which sanctification is effected.

It is very likely that more Christians have lost their faith over this issue than any other. Every pastor has watched and prayed with his suffering people as they struggled with the "why" of their dried-up brook.

Not even the most consecrated Christian can be insulated from shock and grief when loved ones are taken by death. But they can be prepared ahead of time so that their faith will not give way under the stress of loss.

The secret is to rest upon the assurance that God will not permit any circumstance that is not for our best good. This requires faith, but it is not difficult to trust the One who died for us. We must keep on reminding ourselves that God will allow many situations which will seem to us like terrible tragedies. We will not be able to discern any logic or reason behind the events. Our human faculties may rebel at the very thought that any good could ever result from such circumstances.

Here is where we must cling to the Word of God and nothing else. This is the dividing place between the mature and immature Christian. The loss will either drive us closer to Jesus, or cause us to turn from Him. At this point, everything depends upon the personal relationship which has been developed prior to the crisis. Those who have understood and accepted the principle that God's love

will not allow any trial which is not for
our best good—only they will be able to
relate properly to the experience.

Reasons for Trusting

We have said that faith alone will
hold us in this kind of traumatic test.
Nevertheless, our faith is not blind or
unreasonable. We have a fabulous reservoir of experiences with God which
prove His unfailing love and concern for
us. Why should this one be any different?
Even though I can't understand it, I can
trust Him who has promised. If His Word
has never failed before, how could it fail
in this situation? Then, like Job, we can
say, "Though he slay me, yet will I trust
in him." Job 13:15.

Here we may learn a lesson from the
trustful manner in which parents surren-
der their children into the hands of a
surgeon. How can they submit that be-
loved child to the cutting of that knife and
the throbbing pain which inevitably fol-

lows? Two factors make it easy for them to place such confidence in the doctor. They trust his skill and ability to operate successfully, and they have faith in his wisdom to do the right thing at the right time for the good of their child. They also know that after the temporary suffering is past that the child will be better off than it was before the pain.

If we can trust a human physician who often fails, why is it so hard to trust a divine One who never fails? Probably none of our children would ever choose to be operated on, no matter how serious the condition. It is only because of our greater knowledge of their case that we submit them to the surgery. In the same manner, we would never choose to experience the trials and afflictions which our heavenly Father often allows to come upon us. He understands the case completely and knows that after the passing pain we will be better prepared for a happier future.

And here is a beautiful parallel in that

illustration: Even though I know my child will be greatly improved as a result of the cutting, I still suffer right along with him. I sit up during the long hours of the night, holding his hand and ministering to every possible need.

Don't think for one moment that our wonderful Father in heaven doesn't do the same thing for us. Like a small child we may cry over the pain and blame our Father for allowing the cutting to be done. And like a human parent, God must weep because He has no way to communicate His reason for subjecting us to the pain. It is just as impossible for us to understand God's decision for our lives as it is for our children to comprehend our decisions for them.

I think it would be an overwhelming revelation to see ourselves without God's mysterious permissions, painful though they be. Only when we see Jesus face to face and reason on the plane of immortality will we be able to thank Him for allowing things to be just exactly as they were.

I can look back upon certain shatter-
ing experiences in my past and recognize
how they altered the entire direction of
my life. It is easy for me to see how any
significant change in those disappointing
events could have sent me in a totally
opposite direction. I tremble to think
what my life might now be had God not
measured out to me those bitter experiences.

Chosen from Eternity

If indeed the hardships are necessary
to prepare us for entrance into heaven,
then they should be looked upon as a part
of God's great election plan for our salvation. Isaiah wrote, "Behold, I have
refined thee, but not with silver; I have
chosen thee in the furnace of affliction."
Isaiah 48:10.

What a difference it makes in our
attitude if we can see suffering as a sign of
God's special choice for us to spend
eternity with Him. He loved us before we

were born, and according to Paul, "He hath chosen us in him before the foundation of the world, that we should be holy and without blame before him in love." Ephesians 1:4.

Can you fathom the exciting reality of that truth? You are one upon whom the eye of God has rested from eternity. Through all those eons of time, divine Wisdom has been perfecting a detailed plan for your sanctification and ultimate salvation. As you submit to Him, He will certainly perform only what has been determined as absolutely essential to carry out His plan for your life. If that plan allows for heartaches here and there, and even apparent disasters from time to time, God will never permit more than we can bear. He will be there to measure and temper the furnace according to our strength and according to our need.

Does that sound like a contrived explanation for the problem of pain and affliction? It will, no doubt, to the person who does not believe in the existence of

God. He scoffs at the idea that a loving, omnipotent Deity would not intervene to spare His followers from all trouble and pain. Often the believer is hard-pressed to justify the apparent arbitrary manner in which some suffer and some are spared. How can we respond to the accusation that a just God would protect all His people from all trouble at all times?

First of all, let us concede that God could do that very thing. He has the power to prevent accidents. He could commission angels and the Holy Spirit to override the law of cause and effect in the lives of all Christians. They would not get bad colds, stub their toes, or contract cancer.

What would be the effect of such a program? The answer is obvious. Everyone would rush into the Christian camp in order to be protected from trouble in the flesh. The world would literally be compelled to follow Christ for purely physical reasons. God doesn't build His kingdom upon appeals to such motives.

It seems logical that God had to allow the natural laws to operate equally upon all to demonstrate the unconditional nature of His love. Christians do inherit the same genetic weaknesses as others who have no faith. They have accidents, and often die of the very same diseases which assail the unbeliever.

Physically, then, is there any difference in the way Christians suffer, and the way non-Christians suffer? The answer to that question must be carefully qualified. God reveals no partiality in the way He permits natural law to affect all mankind. Any difference which enters the picture must be based upon the individual's response rather than any difference God makes between categories or classes. This is another way of saying that no one in the world can prevent troubles coming into his life, but he can decide what those troubles do to his life after they happen.

The Christian meets trouble by surrendering to the will of God and praying for a spirit to profit from whatever God permits. Such a trusting faith can not only bring power to bear the suffering with less trauma, but also, in some cases, to be healed of the affliction as well. This response of God to the faith of an individual has nothing to do with favoring a class of people. God is still operating within the framework of law, but this time spiritual law instead of natural. That law is not limited to any nationality, race, or religion. All who approach Him in faith will tap into the same reservoir of divine power. Even though God's love is unconditional, His healing power is not. Nevertheless, the conditions are the same for all, and He delights to set the spiritual laws of asking, believing, and receiving into operation for anyone.

Here, then, lies the most understandable human explanation for the mysterious way some are afflicted and others are not. Some are delivered and healed, while others suffer and die. God has to deal with each individual on the basis of that person's faith and the kind of prayer he offers. If his greatest concern is for God to mold him and prepare him for heaven, his prayer will be for God to shape all the circumstances of his life to that end. In order to answer such a prayer of faith, God may have to permit experiences of pain or affliction.

Again, God will have to answer that prayer according to His omniscient knowledge of the future of that individual. Only One who accurately foresees the consequence of every act can safely be trusted to control the circumstances of life.

Is it hard to submit to a God who does not always explain His omniscient actions? Indeed, it would be impossible to trust Him if we had no other subjective evidences of His commitment to our happiness. But anyone who believes that Jesus was willing to die in his place would have to believe also that Jesus would always work for his best good. God would have to deny His own nature

the first time the bird used its wings to fly around the laboratory room. Around and around went the pigeon, excited and panting. Finally, in utter exhaustion, the frantic bird crashed into a wall and fell to the floor seriously injured. Only then did the scientist realize that the pigeon had inherited the instinct to fly but not to stop its flight. Had it not been willing to risk the shock of a crash landing, the bird would have died of stress in midair.

Sometimes God has to stop people from their furious pace before they destroy their own usefulness. The trauma of a sudden stop may be hard to understand and accept. Sickness, loss of job, or even tragedy may be necessary in order to provide time for physical and spiritual recuperation. "Be still, and know that I am God." Psalms 46:10. In the thoughtful hours and days of slow recovery from surgery, many have found the secret of life in Christ.

Perhaps only God understands why pain is often the only thing which can get

the attention of human beings. Never
should we blame God for utilizing the
one device which will ultimately draw us
to Him. Strange as it may seem, prosperity, good health, and smooth sailing
do not attract the soul to God. A man was
imprisoned in a tower and was trying to
alert passersby of his dilemma. They
could not hear his cries, so he began to
drop gold coins from his pocket to attract
their attention. But although they
scrambled about to recover all the falling
money, not one pedestrian looked up to
see the plight of the prisoner. Finally, he
managed to break off a chunk of mortar
from the crumbling wall and dropped it
out the window. It struck a man on the
head, injuring him. Only then did the
man look up and get the message from
above.

In the same way all manner of blessings are taken for granted. Instead of
looking to the source, we are busily gath-
ering more from the world around us. It
is only when we are hurt that we look up

and begin to listen to the message God has been trying to communicate.

Looking for the Reasons

After a period of test, will God always reveal the reasons for His divine permissions in our lives—His dried-up brooks? Eventually, yes. But not necessarily in this life. Our faith may have to hold us steady until God can explain to us, face to face, why it had to be. Paul finally came to know why God allowed his thorn in the flesh. It was to keep him from feeling exalted over the abundance of revelations granted him. I may have to wait until Jesus comes to understand why my little eight-year-old son suffered so long before dying of a brain tumor.

It took a few years for the citizens of Coffee County, Alabama, to understand why the boll weevil invaded their fields, devastating the cotton industry completely. After turning to diversified farming and eventually doubling their income from growing peanuts, the farmers of Coffee County erected a monument to the boll weevil. In the memorial inscription, credit is given to the boll weevil for forcing the change of crops, creating unprecedented prosperity for that area.

Christians should look for the reason when trials appear. Usually, a new door will open when one brook dries up. But if the years bring no satisfactory explanation of tragic loss, then we should trust Him still. Someday He will make it plain to us. In the meantime, we are sustained by the comfort of the One who fully understands our griefs and sorrows. Jesus became one of us so that He could experience every pain and be a faithful Intercessor for us. Only those who have passed through the same suffering can truly sympathize and communicate with our hearts. When one grief-stricken father cried out, "Where was God when my son was killed in that car accident?" the answer quietly came back, "He was exactly where He was when His Son was tortured and killed on the cross."

Isn't there a tremendous lesson in that answer? If God would not intervene to save His own Son's life because He saw that great good would eventually result, then He must have seen some future good when He allowed my son to die also. And is that not the reason I could feel the sweet, personal touch of the Father upon my life during those dark hours of grief? He knew exactly how I felt. He could minister to me as no human friend could do. Has not my own ability to provide healing comfort been greatly strengthened because I have shared a similar sorrow with those who have lost children?

Christians should have no illusions about the source of afflictions. Sin is the cause of all suffering in the world today. God is often blamed for doing the devil's work. Not one cancer has ever been caused by God. In the experience of Job we have a perfect picture of Satan's mis- chievous program to afflict God's faithful children. Up to certain limits God allowed Job to be tested by the great adversary, and the triumphant conclusion of the story reveals why God permitted things to go as far as they did. Job emerged from the devastating trials with a stronger faith and greater prosperity than he had before.

There may be many reasons that God allows Satan limited access to His followers, but one of the chief positive effects is to keep Christians constantly on guard against sin. Through the exercise of a wide-awake conscience, the first approach of our cunning enemy can be recognized and repulsed. The knowledge that he is apt to attack at any moment or place develops a healthy spirit of alert defensiveness.

The story is told of one old Cape Cod fisherman who always hauled in the most sought-after catch of the entire fleet. Because his fish were so lively and healthy, they invariably commanded the highest prices in the marketplace. In vain did the other fishermen try to uncover the secret of his success. Only after his death was the formula revealed by his son, and it was as simple as it was effective. After securing his load of fish safely in the holding tank, the old fisherman would loose several pugnacious catfish into the tank. The constant fear of attack kept all the commercial fish in agitated motion, preserving them from the normal lethargic state brought on by prolonged captivity. Their obvious alertness made them the most desirable in the eyes of the buyers.

Can we not see in this story a possible reason for our own harassment by the wily Satan? Does God allow him to threaten us so that we might be constantly in a protective stance? Perhaps this provocation is exactly what we need to produce a necessary attitude of vigilance.

In the days of the Napoleonic wars, before radio or telegraph had been invented, messages had to be sent by semaphore signals. Even from a long distance the flags could be deciphered as they slowly spelled out words letter by letter. It was by this method that the Battle of Waterloo was reported to the anxious citizens of London.

For years Napoleon had struggled to bring Europe to his feet. Finally his goal was in sight and only the thin, red line of Highlanders stood in his way at Waterloo. The banks of England had poured every available pound into government loans to defeat Napoleon. If the Battle of Waterloo was lost, Britain would be lost.

On the coasts of Dover the people of London gathered to watch for news of the battle. Suddenly they saw across the channel the big semaphore begin to move. Painfully slow, the letters began to form into the first words of a message: "W-E-L-L-I-N-G-T-O-N D-E-F-E-A-T-E-D." Then suddenly, a dense fog settled over the scene and blotted out the signals. But the people had seen enough to convince them that their general had been put to rout. In despair they fled the city. Raw militia rushed to the coast prepared to die in desperate hand-to-hand combat with

THE BROOK DRIED UP   31

the expected invasion force. Road blocks
were erected and houses hastily fortified.

For two days London resigned itself
to destruction. Then the storm abated and
the fog began to lift. Watchers saw the
semaphore flags begin to move once more,
and the message was slowly spelled out:
"W-E-L-L-I-N-G-T-O-N   D-E-F-E-A-
T-E-D N-A-P-O-L-E-O-N A-T W-A-
T-E-R-L-O-O." The joy of the people
knew no bounds as the full import of the
news struck home.

Living in a world that is often ob-
scured by tears and human misunder-
standing, we do not always have access to
the whole truth.   Like the despairing
Londoners, we are not able to see past the
apparent tragedies of His interrupted
message.   When the fog of unbelief is
lifted and the veil is completely taken
away, we will recognize for the first time
that there was no defeat at all. It had been
victory from the very beginning, but we
just didn't have the rest of the message.
The whole message will be understood

only when Jesus Himself speaks to us beyond the mist of our limited human view.

In the meantime, what is the solution? The solution, my friend, is simply to trust the promise of One who has never failed us yet. "And we know that all things work together for good to them that love God, to them who are the called according to his purpose." Romans 8:28.